"Ms. Goal Digger," the title itself is a sensational play on words! This guide to claiming your success, anchoring your power position, and securing your indelible legacy will be your most used asset in your arsenal to "have it all..." Ms. Vaughn's approach to "sexy" success is the quintessence of who she is; delightful, honest, authentic, charming, savvy, and efficacious. She is such an inspirational role model, helping many change their lives while achieving great success in her many roles with elegant, style and class. Thank God, she graciously shares how we can achieve the same in her must-have-how-to-guide!

~Carole Gist, M.Ed., Miss USA 1990

Ms. Goal Digger is a must read for every woman striving to live her best life in business. It's an investment in yourself that is purposeful and profitable, and the dividends can be passed on for generations. It's a daily go-to-guide for everyone!

Gail Perry-Mason
Financial Coach and Founder of Money Matters for Youth
Author of *Girl, Make Your Money Grow*!

I have known Alison since we were both fresh out of college and she has always been passionate about empowering women to live their best lives. Goal-setting is the buzzword in the business these days and Alison is fantastic with throwing light on how to approach your goals strategically, how to dress like a CEO and how to effectively network. The tips she has put together in this book will help anyone overcome obstacles to their success.

-Shaun Robinson
Emmy Award-winning journalist,
TV Personality, Philanthropist
Author of *Exactly As I Am*

MS. GOAL DIGGER

MS. GOAL DIGGER

SUCCESS IS SEXY - A CEO'S GUIDE TO GOAL SETTING,
DRESSING THE PART AND HAVING IT ALL

Alison Vaughn

Ms. Goal Digger: A CEO's Guide to Goal Setting, Dressing the Part and Having it All!
Copyright © 2017 by Alison Vaughn
www.AlisonVaughn.com
ISBN: 1542506018
ISBN 13: 9781542506014
Library of Congress Control Number: 2017900551
CreateSpace Independent Publishing Platform
North Charleston, South Carolina

Edited by So It Is Written LLC www.soitiswritten.net

Printed in the United States of America

DEDICATION

This book is dedicated to my beautiful, elegant, sophisticated mother, Betty; and my energetic daughter, Sarah. Thank you, God, for the vision to help others reach their goals.

Building an empire, leaving a legacy!

ACKNOWLEDGEMENTS

THANK YOU TO my inspiration: The Father, the Son and the Holy Spirit. I would like to thank my mother, "Ms. Betty" as many call her. She is my rock, my role model and inspiration for so many things. Thank you to the Jackets for Jobs employees for embracing my God-given vision to empower individuals entering the workforce. Tenita Johnson, thank you for the insight and support in bringing this project to fruition and Pam Perry for all of your guidance.

Last, but certainly not least, thank you to my Fellowship Chapel Family and everyone who offered a generous smile or an avenue for assistance. The seeds you've sown do not go unnoticed.

TABLE OF CONTENTS

INTRODUCTION

THE URBAN DICTIONARY defines *goal digger* as a person who desires wealth in all areas of life; one who seeks the secrets of the millionaire mind; one who has the smarts, optimism, integrity, and passion to do it themselves. Merriam-Webster's Learner's Dictionary defines *gold digger* as a woman who becomes or tries to become romantically involved with a rich man in order to get money and gifts from him.

There's a huge difference between a *goal digger* and a *gold digger*. Gold diggers will never truly become successful. They will never be happy; they will always live in someone else's shadow. Goal diggers, however, are the opposite. They will be the happiest people you can find, and thus, the most successful.

Goals are extremely instrumental for success. When you accomplish your goals, you feel better about yourself.

This book focuses on being independent and getting what you want for yourself, by yourself.

In addition to tips on etiquette and networking, I will show you how to set goals, how to dress like a CEO and how to get and stay motivated every day.

As part of my research for this book, I'm listening intently to the lyrics of Kanye West's song, "Gold Digger." I wanted to hear a man's perspective of a gold digger so I wouldn't steer you in that direction. While I love the beat of his song, I want you to dance to a different beat.

In this book, I will list some motivational songs for women that will uplift, motivate and jumpstart your day. I guarantee that you will love my playlist!

Thank you for your patronage, while investing in your future!

A WOMAN who walks in PURPOSE doesn't have to chase PEOPLE or OPPORTUNITIES. Her LIGHT causes PEOPLE and OPPORTUNITIES to PURSUE her.

CHAPTER 1

TOUCHED BY BILLIONAIRES

As THE CEO of an award-winning non-profit organization, *Jackets for Jobs*, I have secured millions of dollars for my company, formed great partnerships, traveled the world, and have been favored by many billionaires.

In 2000, I had a "God idea" to empower women to enter the workforce. In 2002, the great city of Detroit embraced my vision and we joined forces to help Detroiters gain employment. In 2007, I formed a partnership with TJ Maxx, the largest international apparel and home fashions off-price department store chain in the United States. When Jackets for Jobs and TJ Maxx formed a partnership, TJ Maxx invested one million dollars to the company. Our partnership allowed Jackets for Jobs to expand its services to also assist men who were looking to enter the workforce. After 16 years, Jackets for Jobs has helped over 20,000 job seekers secure employment. It has been a blessing to touch so many lives. TJ Maxx is a billion-dollar company that believes in giving back to the community. However, working with TJ Maxx was not my first billionaire experience.

In 2002, I had the honor of being a guest on *The Oprah Winfrey Show*. Being a guest on her show was a dream come true. All of my friends and family witnessed this monumental moment. This was my first "Touched by a Billionaire" experience. *Forbes* magazine listed Oprah as the first black female billionaire. The topic of the particular show I appeared on was makeovers. As you can imagine, being a guest on her show was unbelievable. From the limo ride to the studio, the mouth-watering, all-you-can-eat refreshments in the green room, to the friendly staff that assisted me before, during and after the show, it was truly a time to treasure. Oh, and the gifts! After my makeover, I received a hair, nail and spa package to a glitzy salon in Chicago.

A year later, ABC's *The View* did a nationwide search for the best hometown hero and charity. My team created a video on Jackets for Jobs and submitted the video to ABC. Thousands applied, but only four charities won. We were one of the four to win money and recognition! I've always admired Barbara Walters; to be on her show was another dream come true. Star Jones interviewed me and, years later, she spoke for Jackets for Jobs. We promoted her book, *Satan's Sisters*.

The year 2005 was one of my favorite years. God really had His hand on me. I graduated from Word of Faith Laypersons Bible School. While receiving national attention from being on *The Oprah Winfrey Show*, which was great, appearing on NBC's *Today Show* was epic! Each year, Al Roker airs a segment called, "Lend a Hand." He searches nationwide for charities to support and lend a hand. Well, who do you think he selected? Yes, Jackets for

Jobs! He flew to Detroit and broadcasted live all morning from my office. More than half the show was dedicated to my mission to help empower women. Not only did we talk about Jackets for Jobs' mission, but NBC graced us with plenty of gifts. Millions of viewers watched as Al presented the grand finale gift: a van courtesy of Toyota. On our company's website, we keep a wish list of things we need. At that time, a van was one of the items we needed for donation pickup.

Later that same year, I was touched by billionaire, Donald Trump. In the 2016 Presidential Election, the country elected him as our 45th President of the United States. Cast members from Donald Trump's hit NBC TV show, *The Apprentice,* wanted to give back and make a difference in the community. They created a calendar in which proceeds from the calendar would go to a specific charity. Who do you think they selected? Yes, they selected Jackets for Jobs! Donald Trump liked the idea, and he wrote Jackets for Jobs a check. My company is now listed in his checkbook. This was yet another life-changing billionaire experience.

My mother and I flew to New York to meet the cast members, and the event was featured on page 6 of the *New York Post.* I'm setting the stage to let you know, I'm on to something. Oprah, Donald Trump, *The View, The Today Show*…take note! Charm, etiquette and networking all play important roles in success. This book reveals my strategies.

In 2006, I had the distinct honor of ringing the closing bell on NASDAQ, a position reserved for coveted CEOs. The Nasdaq Stock Market is an American stock exchange. It is the second-largest exchange in the world by market capitalization, behind only the New York Stock Exchange. Now, the Lord is moving me beyond millions and billions. We are talking the world stock market. Let's call it trillions. I can't even find the words to express that feeling of being in New York, seeing my company name on the huge jumbotron in the middle of Times Square and hitting that button at the close of day. It was a surreal moment!

Not only did my company ring the closing bell in 2006, but we rang it again in 2014 on World Humanitarian Day. Talk about the favor of God! That was the perfect day for Jackets for Jobs to ring the closing bell because I had just opened an office in Botswana, a country in Southern Africa, therefore officially becoming a global company.

I gained an international presence. One day, I received an email that catapulted me to a different level. I was asked to speak in Dubai, the *City of Luxury*. As the business hub of the Middle East, Dubai is a city in the United Arab Emirates known for luxury shopping, ultramodern architecture, and a lively nightlife scene.

As a keynote speaker at the World Islamic Economic Forum, I spoke about women in the workplace. I had a wonderful, unforgettable experience in Dubai.

I've also had the honor of meeting billionaires Martha Stewart and Dan Gilbert. Martha Stewart is a businesswoman, writer, and television personality. She is the founder of Martha Stewart Living Omnimedia, and has gained much success through a variety of business ventures. I love New York, so when I was asked to join other women entrepreneurs *and* meet Martha Stewart, I was elated! I was honored to receive her *Dreamers into Doers* Award, which is an award Martha presents to women who turn their dreams into reality. Martha has turned her products and services into a billion-dollar industry.

Dan Gilbert earned his billions from his companies, Rock Ventures and Quicken Loans. He also owns the NBA Cleveland Cavaliers. Dan believes in revitalizing Detroit and supports our workforce development mission. Jackets for Jobs is blessed to have financial support from Quicken Loans.

Anyone that knows business, or has thought about investing, definitely knows Warren Buffett. When he speaks, people listen. As a graduate of Goldman Sachs 10,000 Small Businesses Program, Mr. Buffett spoke at our graduation. I had the honor of meeting him and at the conclusion of class, we had mock elections with "Most Likely to…" awards. I received the "Most likely to have lunch with Warren Buffett" Award. I'm putting it in the universe, and we'll see what happens. If it doesn't happen, I'm thankful to have shaken his hand.

God has blessed me, and many people consider me successful. That's why I want to empower you. Success means different things to different people. Success is defined as "the favorable or prosperous termination of attempts or endeavors; the accomplishment of one's goals; the attainment of wealth, position, honors, or the like." Whatever success means to you, I sincerely hope you attain it if you haven't done so already.

Please
and
Thank You

ARE STILL MAGIC WORDS.

CHAPTER 2

ETIQUETTE

TO BE TOUCHED by grace and present yourself with confidence, you must know proper etiquette. According to a study conducted by Stanford Research Institute, Harvard University, and the Carnegie Foundation, 85% of your professional success is attributed to your social skills; only 15% attributed to your technical knowledge. For that reason, I attended and graduated from Charleston School of Protocol taught by Cindy Grosso in Charleston, South Carolina. Secondly, etiquette will provide a good foundation to the following chapters.

Emily Post said, "Good manners reflect something from the inside—an innate sense of consideration for others and respect for self."

Being a female is a matter of birth. Being a woman is a matter of age, but being a lady is a matter of choice.

A lady graciously accepts compliments. She does not downgrade herself, as if she doesn't deserve admiration from other person. She smiles and simply responds, "Thank you."

Always be a lady. Always be charming. Never lower your standards to accommodate another's lack of taste.

FIVE WAYS TO BE CHARMING

1. Saying "Please" & "Thank you!"
2. Practicing good etiquette.
3. Always remembering names.
4. Smiling often.
5. Writing thank-you notes. Find and use your signature stationary.

The words, "please" and "thank you," can spark magic. These words can open doors for you. Here is a southern charm tip from *Southern Living*:

> With introductions, keep the focus on the *person*.
> Example: "This is Claire, my friend from work."
> NOT: "This is my friend from work, Claire."

Entertain as much as possible. I love entertaining and bringing friends and family together. There is never a reason too small to celebrate. When entertaining, be a gracious and lively host. When you go to a party, always take a hostess gift. Flowers are one of the best gifts in token of love, thanks, sympathy or apology. Remember, when giving flowers, place them in a vase so the hostess doesn't have to find one.

When talking to a couple, remember that a man is never separated from his last name. Therefore, a married couple should always be referred to in the following way: "Lisa and John Smith."

A lady always says, "Excuse me," in a polite tone as she moves through a crowded space. She also knows that "I'm sorry" is required only when an apology is in order.

Always respect yourself. If you don't, others won't either. Remember, the world paints an image of you based upon what you put out there. So, hold yourself to a high standard of grace and elegance. Confidence and a smile are your best accessories; never leave home without them. According to Southern charm, never leave home without pearls.

DINING ETIQUETTE

Hosting meetings with food is a great way for potential clients and business colleagues to see your business etiquette skills. The No. 1 rule in dining etiquette is to follow the host's lead. As an image consultant and graduate of Charleston School of Protocol, I could write an entire book on etiquette and image, but I will condense it to a few key etiquette tips:

- Sit up straight.
- Chew with your mouth closed.
- Keep your elbows off the table.
- Do not reach across the table.
- Dab, don't wipe, when using a napkin.

When you're seated at the dinner table, and someone asks you to pass the salt, do you:

A) Pass the salt.
B) Pass the salt and pepper.
C) Tell them to get it themselves.

The correct answer is **B**. Pass the salt and pepper together, even when one or the other is requested.

Table Etiquette

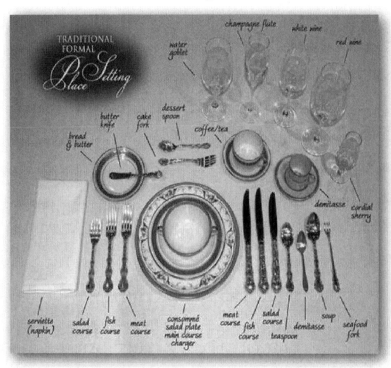

NAPKIN ETIQUETTE

At informal meals, place the napkin in your lap immediately upon seating. If there is a host or hostess, wait for him or her to take their napkin off the table and place it in his or her lap. (An exception to this rule is buffet-style meals, where you should unfold your napkin when you start eating.)

Cutlery. Deciding which knife, fork or spoon to use is easier when you use the outside-in table manners rule: use the utensils on the outside first, working your way inward.

Seasoning Food. When attending a dinner party or restaurant, proper table manners dictate that you taste your food before seasoning it. Bread is most often placed on the table in a basket that everyone shares.

- If the bread is placed in front of you, feel free to pick up the basket and offer it to the person on your right.
- If the loaf is not sliced, slice a few pieces and offer them to the person to your left, then pass the basket to your right.
- Do not touch the loaf with your fingers. Instead, use the cloth in the bread basket as a buffer to steady the bread as you slice it.
- Place the bread and butter on your butter plate. Your butter plate is on your left. Break a bite-sized piece of bread, put a little butter on it, and eat it.

- Don't butter the whole piece of bread and take bites from it.
- Don't hold your bread in one hand and a drink in the other.
- Don't take the last piece of bread without first offering it to others.

Excusing Yourself. Simply say, "Excuse me, please. I'll be right back," when leaving for the restroom. Leaving without saying a word is rude.

Cutting Food. Cut your food into only one or two bite-sized pieces at a time.

Electronic Devices. Turn off or silence all electronic devices before entering the restaurant. If you forget to turn your cell phone off, and it rings, immediately turn it off. Do not answer the call. Do not text or browse the Internet while at the table.

Elbows. The "no elbows on the table" rule applies only when you are actually eating. When no utensils are being used, placing your elbows on the table is acceptable.

Holding a Wine Glass. White wine glasses are held by the stem, not the bowl. Red wine glasses may be held by the bowl.

WINE TASTING ETIQUETTE

Once wine is poured into the proper glass, it's time to evaluate and enjoy the wine. Evaluating wine involves four basic steps: looking, swirling, smelling and tasting.

- **Step #1 – Look.** Hold the wine glass up against a white background, such as a napkin or table cloth, to evaluate its color and clarity. Red wines should range in color from deep purple to brick red. White wines should range in color from lemon gold to golden amber.
- **Step #2 – Swirl.** Swirl the wine in your glass to aerate it.
- **Step #3 – Smell.** Put your nose in the glass and take a deep breath. Older wines should have subtler aromas than younger ones.
- **Step #4 – Taste.** For proper wine tasting, fill your mouth about half full, and subtly swish the wine around.

TIPPING ETIQUETTE - RESTAURANTS

The usual tip is 15 to 20% on the pre-tax amount of the bill. Here are extra tip points to consider by category:

- **Self-Service Restaurants**: 10%
- **Stellar Service from Waiters:** Add an extra $5 for extra special service
- **Lingering at Your Table on a Busy Night:** Add an extra 10-15%
- **Bartenders**: Tip 15-20% of the total bill

Note: Tip discreetly. Tipping is a private matter.

PHONE ETIQUETTE

CHOOSE A NORMAL RINGTONE.
You don't want people to hear music blaring each time your phone rings. Even your ringtone should be professional.

LET THE PERSON ON THE OTHER END OF THE PHONE KNOW WHEN YOU HAVE THEM ON SPEAKERPHONE.
If you must put someone on speaker phone, make sure you immediately let them know before doing so.

DON'T LEAVE LONG VOICEMAILS.
Leave a short, straightforward message. If you leave your phone number, be sure to pronounce each number clearly and slowly.

OBSERVE THE 10-FOOT PROXIMITY RULE.
Keep a distance of at least 10 feet from the nearest person when talking on a cell phone.

DON'T BLAME THE OTHER PERSON FOR A DROPPED CALL.
Saying, "I think your phone must have dropped the call" sounds petty and could possibly hurt someone's feelings.

LOWER YOUR VOICE WHEN TAKING CALLS IN PUBLIC.
There's so much to say regarding etiquette. Etiquette, integrity and character are the foundational bricks for

building your empire. Proverbs 10:9 says, *"She who walks with integrity walks securely."*

- Remember to speak with honesty, think with sincerity, and act with integrity.
- Integrity is not something you show others. It's how you behave behind their back.
- People with good intentions make promises; however, people with good character keep them.
- Character exemplifies what you really are. Your reputation is what others think you are.
- No matter how educated, talented, rich or cool you believe you are, how you treat people ultimately tells all. Integrity is everything.
- Character is how you treat those who can do nothing for you.

I love my career! Jackets for Jobs provides career skills training, employment etiquette training, in addition to clothing for job seekers. Everyone who walks through our doors has some sort of hardship or disadvantage to entering the workforce. The employees and volunteers all have great character. They treat everyone, including those people who can't do anything for them, with dignity and respect.

THINGS MONEY CAN'T BUY:

- Character
- Manners
- Morals
- Respect
- Common Sense
- Trust
- Patience
- Class
- Integrity
- Love

"Class is an aura of confidence that is being sure without being cocky. Class has nothing to do with money. It is self-discipline and self-knowledge."

ANN LANDERS

Set some goals on how you can improve the way you do things with style & grace

_____

_____

_____

_____

_____

_____

_____

_____

_____

_____

_____

_____

_____

_____

_____

_____

_____

_____

_____

_____

_____

_____

_____

_____

_____

_____

"Your smile is your *logo*, your personality is your *business card*, how you leave others feeling after an experience with you is your *trademark*."

CHAPTER 3

REMEMBERING NAMES AND BUSINESS CARD ETIQUETTE

DALE CARNEGIE SAID, "If you remember my name, you pay me a subtle compliment; you indicate that I have made an impression on you. Remember my name and you add to my feeling of importance." According to Dr. Ellen Weber, through PET scans when someone's name is spoken in their presence, a part of the brain that processes "self" lights up. Dr. Weber states, "Research confirms you also spark their brain's sense of worth, and add value to their day." I am astounded and amazed by Dale Carnegie's intuitive intelligence.

Do you want to add value to someone's day by saying their name when you greet them, but have trouble remembering their name? Have you ever been introduced to someone and a moment later, their name escapes your memory? If you've ever spent the remainder of the event or evening avoiding that person because of the possibility of having to introduce them to someone else, you know how embarrassing this can be.

Don't worry. Difficulty remembering names is very common. We often miss someone's name when we are introduced to them because we are subconsciously focused on making an impression at that moment. We aren't focused on the other person, so we never even get their name.

However, remembering names is important, both in our business and our social lives. When someone learns and remembers our name, we feel special. We think highly of that person because he or she makes us feel valued.

Here are some tips to help you better remember names:

1. When you are introduced in a business setting, give the person your full attention. Repeat the name as soon as you hear it, and try to visualize it written on a piece of paper. Use the name in the introduction. For example, "It's nice to meet you, Mr. Adams."
2. Introduce yourself clearly. Pause between your first and last name. Chances are, people will say their names more clearly as well.
3. Make sure you get it! If you didn't catch the person's name, ask them to repeat it. Say it after them to make sure you have it.
4. Ask for help. If the name is unusual or difficult to pronounce, ask the person to pronounce it correctly. They will feel flattered that you care.
5. Use visual aids. Check the name tag and business card. Seeing a name in print makes it easier to

remember. Keep a notebook handy; write down the name as soon as you can.

6. Rule of 3: Use the name three times in conversation: *Nice to meet you, Steve, Where are you from, Steve?* and *It's been a pleasure talking with you, Steve.*
7. At a business event, pin your name tag on your right shoulder. When shaking hands with someone, people naturally turn slightly and they will see your name tag easily. If you can't see their name tag, you can ask about it in a humorous way. Seeing their name will help you remember it.

Now, go out and add value to someone's day by saying their name when you greet them!

In the United States, exchanging business cards is usually a very casual act. However, this does not hold true everywhere in the world. If your work causes you to interact with foreign professionals, find out the proper way to hand out your business card before you start networking. As the business world grows ever more internationally, it is increasingly important to understand the cultures and customs of other nations.

Asian translated business cards are always exchanged with two hands (as a sign of respect). Asian business cards represent the person to whom you are being introduced, so it's polite to study the card for a while. Then, put it on the table next to you or in a business card case. To attend a meeting without a translated Asian business card causes almost irreparable damage to the business relationship; it is tantamount to refusing to shake hands at a Western business meeting. Before presenting your business card, make sure your card includes your title, that it is clean and neat--no dog-eared corners or smudges allowed. If your company is the oldest or largest in your country, that fact should be on your card, as well.

Your business cards for China, Japan or Korea should be bilingual, even if the people you are meeting understand the English language.

Exchanging business cards in Japan is practically a ceremonial occasion. It is acceptable to offer your business card with just one hand; however, you must always receive a business card with both hands. Status remains to be very important in Japanese culture. So, if you endeavor to make a truly good first impression, ensure that your title is prominently displayed on your business card.

If you are seated in a business meeting with Japanese people who gave you their business cards, it is considered as a mark of respect to place their cards in front of you at the table until the conclusion of the meeting. (This is also a great trick to remember names!)

In Korea, business persons should always have their Korean bilingual business cards ready. Treat the exchange of Korean-translated business cards with respect.

It is best to stand when exchanging Asian business cards. When presenting your business cards, make sure you hold it with the translated side up, facing your contact, so he or she can read it.

In the business world in India, there is great emphasis on academic achievement. If you do business in India, consider adding your own academic achievements to your business card. Also remember that in India, as well as most of the Middle East, you should offer a business card with the right hand, even if you are a lefty.

I want you to have a global mindset. As a former employment representative, hiring flight attendants for a global airline, I have traveled the world. Knowing these tips really helped me in my travels.

HUSTLE UNTIL YOUR HATERS ASK IF YOU ARE HIRING.

CHAPTER 4

SETTING GOALS AND VISION BOARDS

You can't win the race if you don't know where the finish line is. It may sound trite, but it's true. Oftentimes, people work – and work hard – without a clear understanding of where they are going. It's not very productive, nor is it fair.

Think of yourself as a young employee just entering the workforce, or a nervous volunteer. Can you remember the frustration when you didn't understand what was going on around you? Remember when you didn't know what to do? You felt so uncomfortable. That sort of anxiety isn't necessary. Replacing that emotion with exhilaration and determination would feel better.

Before you set goals, you need a clear idea of your mission. Becoming rich is not a goal; five million dollars in three years is a goal.

People who set goals are much more likely to accomplish them than those who don't. Be one of those people and accomplish your aspirations. You don't need more time. We all have 24 hours in a day; the problem is how we manage our 24 hours. All of us dream about a better life, job, relationship or income. In order to turn our imaginations, dreams and aspirations into real accomplishments, we have to take uncommon actions.

We all have desires, dreams and wishes. But until they become clearly-defined goals, they are only that — dreams and wishes. Goal-setting programs suggest starting with the end in mind. A vision board, a visual representation of your end result, will help you stay focused regarding your goals. A well-designed vision board enables you to clearly see "your future" and allows your subconscious mind to lead you there. Meanwhile, your conscious mind has something tangible to focus on as you plan your action steps and move forward.

SAMPLE VISON BOARD

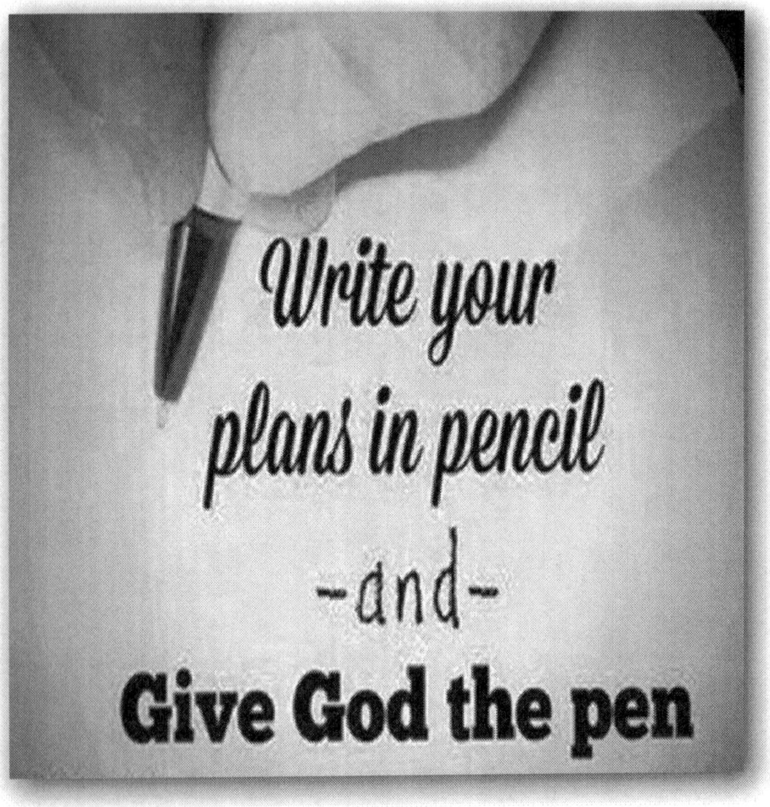
Write your
plans in pencil
-and-
Give God the pen

CHAPTER 5

THE DEFINITION OF A VISION BOARD

A VISION BOARD is a specific Law of Attraction success tool. Simply stated, the Law of Attraction is the ability to attract into our lives whatever we are focusing on. It can be used as a powerful, life-transforming blueprint that guides you in achieving your goals and dreams. It's a tool that quickly and easily reprograms your powerful subconscious mind. It is also known as a treasure map, dream board or goal board. A vision board provides you with long-term, sustainable results. Vision boards became extremely popular after John Assaraf's story about his vision board success was highlighted in *The Secret*. John was living in his dream home and he didn't even realize that he had bought the exact same house that was on his goal boards because the boards were packed away in boxes for years.

How to Make a Vision Board

Traditionally, a vision board or treasure map is a work of art; it's a collage of well-chosen images, words and phrases arranged in a pleasing manner and glued to a poster board. Your life is a "work of art" and you are the alchemist of your life!

Create your own vision board. It's a wonderful, creative way to put your goals and dreams on paper. We all have different learning profiles, which are a combination of auditory, visual and kinesthetic.

When you translate your dreams and put them on a vision board, this gives you an opportunity to physically interpret them. This also brings you a step closer to achieving them.

For the next few weeks, gather pictures, colors, articles and sayings that you like. Don't analyze your choices. If you like what you see or read, cut it out and keep it.

Then, set aside a time where you are relaxed and won't be disturbed. Spread everything you have collected out in front of you. Imagine you are going to create a collage. Look at all the different pictures, colors and sayings in front of you. Pick up whatever catches your eye first and place this on your vision board. Again, there is no right or wrong here. It may need to be placed in the center of the board, or in the top right-hand corner. Choose the best location for each piece.

Fill your vision board with the remaining items you collected. These items aren't just random pictures and colors. They represent your thoughts, your dreams and your aspirations. Your creation won't make sense to another person; your dreams and goals are specific to you and you only.

When your board is complete, stand back and observe it as a complete picture. This is your story. This is who you are and where you want to go.

> # Think of yourself as a human magnet, constantly attracting what you speak, think and feel.

Choose a place to hang the vision board. It needs to be located in a place where you will see it often. Each time you pass it, you will be gently reminded of your dreams and aspirations for the future.

You have given yourself permission to think about your goals and dreams. When your goals are inside your head, they get tucked away in the back of the "filing cabinet." Sometimes, the "key" gets lost or thrown away.

Your dreams are now on full display on your vision board. It could also be called an honesty board. Each picture or word on the board has been carefully selected. The honesty board forces you to ask yourself, "What do I really want here?" What you say you want and what you really want can be very different.

So, have fun. Give it a go. Be inspired, and bring your dreams a step closer to reality by creating your own vision board.

Create a mini-vision board for yourself that inspires you

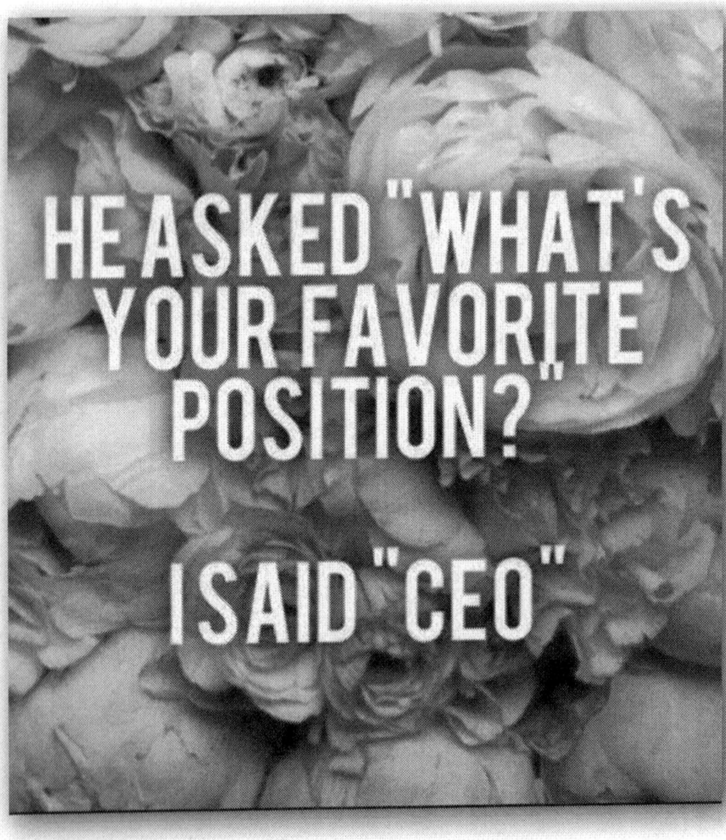
HE ASKED "WHAT'S YOUR FAVORITE POSITION?"
I SAID "CEO"

CHAPTER 6

HOW TO DRESS LIKE A CEO

DRESSING FOR WORK is difficult enough. Dressing like a CEO is even harder. If you're serious about your image, you have to know that it goes beyond your suit. Your desk, your accessories, and even your smartphone's case need to be an extension of your professional image. No matter how much people say they don't judge a person by his or her appearance, it has become more of a human flaw to do exactly the same. At times, it gives an impression that we can't even help it anymore.

One of the most important facets of executive presence is appearance. Appearance is a extraordinarily powerful first filtering. In a corporate setting, you are not defined by whom you report to; the clothes you wear do all the talking. You may slog your backside in the office. But if you aren't dressed for the job you really want, you won't get anywhere. Many professionals and managers won't take you seriously until you change your wardrobe.

Many people may not have the budget to dress for the job they want, although looking like a million bucks is a big deal. Dressing in a similar style as your boss displays your desire to further your career and to have a more executive presence. A new term defined as the "Wow!" factor that makes great leaders stand out. It can get you knocked off the list in a second.

Build Your Wardrobe

Your wardrobe should include season-neutral trousers, a blazer and a pencil skirt. Stick to solid colors like black, navy and gray to switch it up every now and then. If you have a really nice pair of black pants or slacks (slim, flared or wide), you can wear them with a relaxed ivory blouse and boucle jacket for a Chanel-inspired office look.

For a slightly more relaxed office look, you can wear that same pair of pants with a white T-shirt and a colored blazer. For an even more casual look, wear the pants with a long, chunky sweater. If you buy a navy blazer with a black collar, match it with a pair of navy or black pants and a light gray cashmere sweater on the days when you need to look like a boss. When you're going out, accentuate that same blazer with a pair of skinny jeans, sharp stilettos, and a silk, slinky camisole for a super sleek look. You'll still look like a boss, but in a different way.

Necessity is the Mother of Invention

Most startups are open to casual dress, but don't take it lightly. There will be times when you'll be expected to dress formally, so keep a business suit or dress on hand.

However, you can always give it a causal touch by going for more soft colors or wearing blazers that are either self-lined or half-lined for summer months. You can go for a pair of jeans rather than trousers, something like Anne Hathaway in *The Intern*.

Carefully Select Your Color

While you may rock every color, wearing a neon-colored shirt in a meeting is downright obnoxious. You want to make a positive statement with your clothes. They should represent you as a person. Play with colors. Follow the color psychology and decide how you want to be perceived. Dark colors generally depict dominance. Shades of blue inspire confidence in others, and wearing softer colors show a friendlier side of you.

Tailor Everything

You may be wearing an Armani suit, but if it's loose on your shoulders, a little too tight to button, or the pants are a little baggy, you have failed miserably. This is the reason why all the big shots have personal tailors; tailoring can make a huge difference!

An alternative is to buy reasonably priced staples and take them to your tailor! A tailor can nip in a jacket at the waist, slim down the legs of an overly baggy pair of pants, and hem lengths on garments. The tailor cannot easily change shoulders or collars on jackets and crotches on pants, so look out for these areas when shopping.

Wear Modishly

You definitely don't want to be that girl with a Bluetooth piece in your ear all the time, or that person who wears shades when it's dark. Find the right accessories for your personality. A smartwatch will help you in your day-to-day work while making you look advanced with the latest technology. Avoid jangly jewelery, or anything flashy and sparkling. Shine bright like a diamond, but not literally.

Shoes are Great, Too

When you're busy rummaging for that perfect dress or suit, shoes may escape your mind. Do not make this mistake. The dilemma is to walk comfortably or take it up a notch with heels. As painful as heels may be, there's something about heels that exert power and makes you radiate with confidence.

Find Statement Jewelry

Look for a fabulous piece of jewelry that will catch everyone's eye. This doesn't mean the piece has to be big and blingy (although those pieces can be great; J. Crew and Bauble Bar make them quite accessible and budget-friendly). Your statement piece could simply be a strand of pearls. Of course, a pearl necklace is very expensive, but you can purchase great quality imitation or costume pearls. After all, pearls were Margaret Thatcher's secret weapon.

Spend in a Few Staple Sheaths

Sheath dresses are great for work because they are versatile, conservative, and most importantly, low-maintenance. They are also appropriate for pretty much any work environment — from satisfying a strict corporate dress code by pairing with pumps, to blending in at the casual startup office with flat, strappy sandals.

Pencil skirts make another great option, especially when paired with breezy blouses. Although these outfits may take a bit longer to style each morning, the ability to mix-and-match certain pieces to create new outfits will save you money while salvaging your sanity and summer wardrobe.

Pick Fabrics Sagely

Cotton and linen are the best fabric choices for staying comfortable in the humidity and heat. Avoid materials such as silk and polyester during the summer months.

Though a breezy material, any bead of sweat clings to silk for dear life. Therefore, a pit-stain ruining your expensive shirt is practically unavoidable when you're sprinting in 100-degree weather to make it to the office on time. Polyester should be exchanged for another fabric, when possible, as it traps the moisture on your skin instead of absorbing it.

Wear Your Power

We all have different items of clothing that makes us feel powerful and capable. For some, it's a hot pink blazer. For others, it's a navy blue suit or a cashmere cardigan. Wear what makes you feel powerful.

Use the One-Third Rule

I recommend sticking to the One-Third Rule. Buy one-third as many clothes as you do now, but spend three times as much on each item. So instead of buying three pairs of pants at average prices, buy one pair of expensive pants and wear them everywhere.

You need to be aware of every style choice you make, from the coat you wear to where you buy a cup of coffee. The brand of coffee chosen has become a style statement. Your coworkers and friends are just as likely to pick up cues about your aspirations by your coffee selection, as all of the other brands you carry on your personage. If you carry it, then its brand becomes part of yours.

Dress Like You Own The Bank.
Not Like You Need A Loan From It.

Dress how you want to be
ADDRESSED.

SHE TURNS HEADS
WITH ALL HER CLOTHES
ON......
IMAGINE THAT

CHAPTER 7

FROM THE MOUTHS OF MEN

As WOMEN, MANY things may make us feel sexy. A new hairstyle. Flawless makeup. A fresh manicure and pedicure. Even a new black business suit with six-inch stilettos. Whatever makes a woman feel sexy, she'll move hell and high water to make it happen. But, what does the average male define as sexy in a woman?

I surveyed men of various age levels and ethnicities for their opinion. While I captured various answers of different calibers, the consensus was that most men consider a woman who is confident in who she is as the sexiest attribute.

Here are 50 things men consider to be sexy that I captured from our focus group:

1. "It's such an intangible. It's a universal essence—meaning it can be one thing about her or multiple things—like her scent, her look, a feature, her skin, mouth, eyes, hair, intelligence, accomplishments, or even her voice. There's so many things that could make her sexy."

2. "There's nothing that makes a woman sexier than how she carries herself when no one is looking!"

3. "It varies so much. It can be the way she dresses, smiles or even talks. It could be defined by any number of things."

4. "Mystique!"

5. "Neat and natural in appearance. Smart and intimate. Someone who doesn't have to dress half naked to make you want her, but rather engages you in conversation and quality time."

6. "Good intellect!"

7. "When she is fully clothed and still sexy!"

8. "Her mind."

9. "What makes a woman sexy is simple: the love of herself. When she believes that she is amazing, without arrogance. Love, passion, faithfulness and beauty are collateral that comes with it and that, in turn, attracts a man."

10. "There are a lot of things that can make a woman sexy, but I will contend that on the most basic level, a woman that has defined *for herself* what 'being a woman" really means. She subscribes to that daily. That's not only sexy, but truly unique and very special. It's easy to go along with the masses or the status quo, but being unique and true to one's self is extremely sexy. Sexiness starts with being the authentic you and being confident about it."

11. "There are more than one or two features in a woman that make her sexy, from the mind to her body. Her spirituality and demeanor. How she speaks and her education. Honesty and her devotion to her man. The way she takes care of her man, herself, and her home. These are just a few traits that make a woman sexy."

12. "Confidence blended with humility."

13. "What's sexy? Really, it can't be described. You just know it when you see it. It varies from her smile to her intellect."

14. "Her mind—what she says and how she says it."

15. "Intelligence. Sooooo sexxy!"

16. "That look, that smile, that walk. And she can talk a little dirty! BOOM!"

17. "Her conversation and the way she carries herself."

18. "When one carries herself as a lady."

19. "Attitude!"

20. "Intelligence, cooking, personality and legs!"

21. "Dressing classy (showing a little, not a lot)."

22. "Fitness. Intelligence. Confidence. Innocence. Spirituality. High heels. Soft feet. A manicure and pedicure!"

23. "I could describe a lot of superficial (yet attractive) things I notice about women that I personally like. But "sexy" to me is emanated in poise, class, confidence, resilience, posture (both physical and emotional), and character."

24. "Confidence."
25. "Confidence. Intelligence. Energy. Attitude. Positive self-image projection. Spiritual essence. Purpose."
26. "It starts with her smile."
27. "The way she carries herself!"
28. "Her vibe and the way she carries herself. Her walk, talk, and the look in her eye.
29. "The life choices she makes early in her life. I admire a woman that invests in herself first, such as education and self-improvement, before taking on other responsibilities, such as motherhood. A dynamic thinker that does not base her life on materialism, but natural beauty where she can look at herself naked—without make-up or embellishments—and love the person she sees in the mirror. The woman who appreciates every attribute and flaw and allows a man to love the very thing she sees, without exception or excuse. In other words, a woman that has the confidence to love herself first, without vanity, with a humble appeal and a thankfulness for the legacy of beauty within her ancestors bestowed upon her. The measure of a woman is not by the trivial matters of curvatures, shapes, and smiles, but by the elation she brings to a man to respect, love, and learn from her."

30. "Her swag. She can be unattractive. But if her swag is on point, it's all about confidence."
31. "As is the case with beauty, sexy is in the eye of the beholder. So, women don't have to attempt to be sexy. Simply having child-bearing hips makes a woman sexy to me. The same goes for bedroom eyes, extremely high intellect, and a big, pretty smile."
32. "The look of self-confidence!"
33. "There is no one thing. It's a complete package, and it's according to what that man's taste and what he likes!
34. "Her smile!"
35. "The ability to be a real lady. Dressed classy. Mostly natural. Smelling good. With intelligent conversation."
36. "Her intellect, her eyes, the way she keeps herself together—her hair, hands and *toes*. Her attitude toward life in general."
37. "Confidence and grace."
38. "Her spirit."
39. "Personality."
40. "A woman who isn't loud or disrespectful. Someone who is kind, helpful, loving, passionate, intimate, affectionate and thoughtful. She dresses well, smells good, and has phenomenal lips and hips."
41. "Her smile. Her style. Her glamor. Her attention. Her intelligence. No guile."

42. "Confidence."
43. "This wouldn't have been my answer in my youth, but at this point in my life, what's most sexy to me is having an intellectual equal."
44. "Her gentleness and kindness!"
45. "Intelligence and modesty. Be a lady."
46. "That smile!"
47. "Isn't a woman deemed sexy without opening her mouth? How can you tell these long lists of qualities then? Isn't it that she feels sexy and projects her enjoyment and confidence in being a woman in the way she carries herself?"
48. "Sexy is when a man isn't ashamed to take her around his family."
49. "Beautiful and intelligent!"
50. "Her love for God, her family and herself!"

Your body
is what makes
you sexy.
Your smile
is what makes
makes you pretty.
But your personality
is what makes
you beautiful.

Set some goals that would improve your sex appeal.

_____

_____

_____

_____

_____

_____

_____

_____

_____

_____

_____

_____

_____

_____

_____

_____

_____

_____

_____

_____

_____

_____

_____

I now live, feel, and expect an abundance of money.

CHAPTER 8

YOU DESERVE TO BE A MILLIONAIRE

A MILLIONAIRE ISN'T smarter than the average person. Millionaires simply have learned how to understand and develop a good relationship with money, which actually enables them to earn more. They also have the right attitude about their life and their surroundings, inspiring confidence in them.

You have to have social confidence. Being confident around your peers, or even those who earn more than you, is an excellent way to inspire those who have confidence in you--which can open doors, and wallets. It is also important to have a great deal of courage. No one earns a fortune sitting around waiting for it to happen. They have the courage to jump out there and earn the money they've always dreamed about.

Delaying gratification is another habit that can help you obtain your dreams. If you have a bit of money to spend now, and you spend it, you won't have that money to use at a later date. If you can delay your gratification a bit, you can use that money to make more money, which eventually allows you to obtain all you've been dreaming of.

Start Somewhere
Unless you are born into riches, inherit wealth from a family member or strike it rich in the lottery, you have to *earn* money. You don't need to earn a lot of money to become wealthy. It's what you do with that money that matters. If you want to increase your odds of becoming a millionaire, look at some of these methods of making extra money. Implementing just a few of these ideas to your lifestyle can increase your wealth. You can earn an extra $250 free money just by opening a new account with Chase Checking. You have to start somewhere!

Do the Millionaire Math
Do the math on what it takes to hit a million dollars. If you make $50,000 a year, and can figure out how to put away 40 percent of it (that is my savings target), it will take you 50 years of saving $20,000 per year to reach your goal. If you don't do your math, you won't get there because you won't have the right mindset. Math is a universal language.

Earn More, Spend Less
Another and perhaps better, way to look at this is to earn more than you spend. I'm not implying that you deprive yourself from the things you enjoy or live like a monk.

Focus on the value of the things you enjoy. Focus on making big wins to reduce your expenses on non-essentials and things that don't bring you joy. You save a lot of money by not dining out often. This takes the financial tension out of any wasted food and allows you to enjoy the meal more.

Above all else, living within your means is the key to financial success. If you can combine both of these principles-- earning more and spending less--you will be ahead of 95% of the world.

SAVE, SAVE, SAVE!

There is a simple fact that many people miss: you will never grow wealthy if you spend everything you earn. Regardless of how much money you earn, you need to save. Having a cash cushion is nice because it prepares you for unexpected expenses and helps you avoid debt. But there is another reason why saving money is important: because of taxes and other factors, money saved is worth more than money earned!

Another advantage of having a cash savings is the ability to use the money for investments or other large purchases when you come across a good deal. This could be something like an investment property, or a good deal that saves you thousands of dollars on a major purchase. Take advantage of these principles and save, whenever possible.

INVEST

Investing is the best way to grow your wealth. Compound interest has been called the strongest force in the universe;

you want that force to work for you! There are many ways to invest, and you can be successful as long as you make wise investment decisions. Let time and compound interest work for you. Investing in tax-advantaged retirement accounts, such as a 401k or Roth IRA, can help grow your wealth more quickly, especially without the drag of taxes pulling down your investment portfolio. You can also use retirement accounts to shape your taxes, both now and in the future, giving yourself a powerful tool to grow your wealth. Investing can seem intimidating if you haven't started yet. But it doesn't have to be.

DEVELOP YOUR OWN PROCESS

The path to becoming a millionaire becomes easier once you start the process. It all starts with small lifestyle changes. For example, making small adjustments to reduce your fixed monthly expenses can go a long way toward helping you spend less than you earn. As a result, it becomes easier to save a little money each month. Once you have a little cash saved, small emergencies are no longer emergencies. This makes it easier to invest.

You can also set up an automatic savings or investment program. *Out of sight, out of mind* is a great motto when it comes to saving.

However, you also need to know where your money is going. There are a number of excellent free online money management tools to utilize so you can see your income, expenses, and spending patterns in one place. My favorite tool is Personal Capital, which helps you track income, spending and your investments.

Once you are familiar with your spending patterns, you can plan your spending and investing around them to help you reach your goals. After that, it's just a matter of time before you start making money. Even if it takes years or decades, the process really is that simple. Remember, this is not an overnight, get-rich-quick scheme. It takes time and planning.

Start Now

If you want to become a millionaire, you have to start now. If you are not able to save money right now because of debt or other financial obligations, you should work on those issues first. This is a tried and true method for setting up an emergency fund, paying down debt, and investing. Once you've started paying down debt, you can begin your million-dollar journey.

Success always starts in the mind. Self-made millionaires are no brighter or smarter than you; they're just ordinary people doing extraordinary things because they dared to dream and placed their dreams into practice. To acquire the millionaire mindset, you must go beyond your comfort zone. Your vision has to become more 'real' than your current reality.

You also need to recognize that there are different things that motivate you. There is "away from" motivation and "toward" motivation. You may initially work with an "away from" motivation because you want to leave your current job, your current lifestyle, etc. But to sustain and inspire you, that initial "away from" motivation needs to combine with a high level of "toward" motivation. The human brain is a goal-seeking mechanism. It's not enough to solely think about what you don't want. You have to create your own super-powerful sense of how things can be and, therefore, give your subconscious mind clear direction.

THE MILLIONAIRE MINDSET

Napoleon Hill once said, "Poverty and riches are the offspring of thought." The mind is the most powerful resource you have. There are no limitations to what the mind can achieve except those we create ourselves. In order to see a different reality, you must first alter the state of your thoughts. Regardless of their upbringing, the wealthy think a certain way. To become a millionaire, you must adopt the same mindset.

MILLIONAIRES DON'T BELIEVE IN LUCK

Millionaires believe that there is no such thing as luck. They're not waiting for some miraculous event to reward them for what they have not earned. The path to financial freedom requires an ingeniously crafted plan. Wealthy people spend close to 30 hours or more each month studying, planning, researching and sorting out their financial life. They utilize the remainder of the time mapping out action steps to get to the next level. They invest their time and skills wisely, forging relationships, making investments, and ultimately, planting seeds that will bear opportunities that the average person sees as simply luck. They know that the world doesn't owe them anything, so they work for what they want. Most of all, they leave nothing to chance. Millionaires make it a point to guard their life's work. It's fascinating how much money people lose due to bad investments and lack of proper insurance policies. The money you lose can always be recovered, but the time you've wasted cannot. The wealthy understand that time is their *real* asset, so they insure their properties and properly investigate before making monetary decisions. To become a millionaire, you need to lay aside any preconceived notion you might have about luck. Wealth can only be built with calculated effort and opportunities, which comes to those who seek them.

Money is Only a Means to an End

Money is good. In fact, money is great, but money's not everything. The purpose of money is so much greater than simply possessing it. Figure out why you want money, why you need money, and what you will accomplish with it. If obtaining money is the ultimate goal, you become lost after you obtain it and spend it recklessly. You may find yourself in a cycle of making and losing money consistently because you didn't set solid goals. A lot of wealthy people are not sucked in by the materialistic things of life, such as flashy cars, lavish homes, and wild lifestyles. This is not because they are more disciplined (although that counts), but their discipline arises from finding a greater purpose for the wealth they possess.

Millionaires Know the Power of Habits

Most millionaires weren't born rich. They made their millions without a trust fund or inheritance. But to make it, they had to make a conscious effort to develop winning habits. Habits are things we do often without conscious thought or reasoning. It's easy to procrastinate, feel lazy, and waste time. These bad habits, however detrimental, are a result of a complacent upbringing, and almost become second nature before we realize how much harm is done.

Millionaires alter their natural inclinations by forcing themselves into actions that eventually become habits that will lead them into success. The outcome of your life is ultimately a function of the habits over the years. Millionaires acquire as much knowledge as they can. They pursue their passions. They don't waste time or procrastinate. They set short-term and long-term goals, and maintain great business and personal relationships.

Millionaires Understand that Wealth Comes Slowly

No one makes a fortune in a day. Millionaires have a patient mindset. They understand that wealth is built over an extended period of time. To truly become financially free, and create something worthwhile for you and future generations, you need to slowly, yet steadily increase your earnings. You have to save more and make wise investment decisions that will bring long-term gain. There is no short-cut. Even a small misstep can set you back months, even years. Your real asset is your time. Avoid get-rich-quick schemes and other fraudulent practices, and learn the patience of sowing and reaping. The fact that wealth builds slowly does not mean you can't live a comfortable life on your way to millionaire status. On the contrary, the more your finances grow, the more you can afford to live at a higher standard.

MILLIONAIRES FOCUS ON BECOMING WEALTHY

Focus is the secret weapon to achieving your goals. Most people desire to live a financially independent life, but they lack focus. They become distracted by everyday worries, responsibilities and, very soon, their priorities change--so does their focus. Your mind can only tackle the problems you put in the forefront. Millionaires focus on one single goal continuously: becoming wealthy. They build their everyday lives around that goal, not the other way around. To become a millionaire, you have to do the same thing--focus your mind's power on your desire to become wealthy.

Building wealth is a journey. You should not only be concerned about the path, but also about the destination. Take the path to wealth that makes you a better person and teaches you lessons of courage, character and generosity. This is the ultimate millionaire mindset. Becoming a millionaire is less of an act and more of an experience that transforms you into the best version of yourself.

In conclusion, to have a millionaire mindset, you should:

- Develop the habits of millionaires
- Create value; don't believe in luck
- Focus on becoming wealthy
- Understand that you build wealth gradually

List several goals you need to act on to become a millionaire

_____

_____

_____

_____

_____

_____

_____

_____

_____

_____

_____

_____

_____

_____

_____

_____

_____

_____

_____

_____

_____

_____

_____

_____

_____

Be a Standout.

Speak up for what you believe.
Illuminate your talents.
Be true to who you are.

CHAPTER 9

BE A STILETTO IN A ROOM FULL OF FLATS

IN AN OVERCROWDED, hypercompetitive world, the only way to make an impression is to break through the noise.

In truth, you already stand out in some way. If I was to ask your friends to share what comes to mind when they think of you, what would they say? What if I asked your spouse or your child? You know they would have an answer! What adjectives would they use to describe you, and would you like their responses?

Here are a few ways to stand out amongst the crowd:

- **Do things differently.** The "how" is oftentimes so much more important than the "what." Add a special touch of class, elegance, humor or spice that makes common look special.
- **Do different things.** It's easy to stand out when you do something no one else is doing. Beating your

competition is not enough to be better. You have to do something different than they do.

- **Stir emotions; spread happiness.** When you stir positive emotions, spread joy, inspiration or peace of mind, you send a message that there's more to where that came from. And they'll keep coming back for more.
- **Be consistent.** The three aforementioned methods of standing out will work only if you are consistent. Someone once said, "Whatever it is, however seemingly insignificant, if it always happens or never happens, you have created something sticky. You have developed an identity that people can count on and will talk about."

If you asked your customers what comes to mind when they think of you, what would they say? What if we asked your employees, vendors, associates, or a stranger on the street? Would you get a common answer or varied responses? Would their perception of you be accurate? Would it be complete? Would their impressions further your relationship and make them choose you over someone else?

Of course, you hope they all have positive things to say. But, even if their comments are complimentary, they may not be solid enough to build the business. From a marketing perspective, standing out is about much more than making a *good* impression--it's about making the *right* impression.

I had the honor of being the centerfold "Beauty of the Week" for the iconic coffee table magazine, *Jet* Magazine. Every major history maker has graced the cover of this magazine. Being the centerfold model required you to be in a bathing suit. I definitely stood out for millions to see. Before the photo was submitted, I had to ask myself, "Am I making a good impression?" Looking back, I know I did.

How does your market need to perceive you in order to understand the value you offer? What adjectives do you want people to use when they describe you, your company, your product or service? How do prospects need to perceive you in order to choose you over the competition?

What adjectives would you use to describe yourself?

_____

_____

_____

_____

_____

_____

Make your official attributes list. Then ask, "Am I, and are we as a company, making daily impressions in everything we do to communicate and reinforce these desired attributes? Do our habits and behaviors make people think, feel and relate to us? If not, what do we need to do differently, and consistently, to get us there?" Don't just be the one who turns on the lights—be the one who gets in early and gets things done. The example you set will spread quickly.

- Be known for something specific.
- Meeting standards, however lofty those standards may be, won't help you stand out.
- Go above the norm. Be the entrepreneur who is known for turning around struggling employees. Be the business owner who makes a few deliveries a week to personally check in with customers. Be the boss who consistently promotes from within. Be known as the person who responds quicker, acts faster, or who always follows up first.
- Pick a worthwhile mission, and excel at that mission.
- Create your own side project.

Excelling at an assigned project is expected. Excelling at a side project helps you stand out. The key is to take a risk with a project, and make sure your company or customers don't share that risk. To succeed, your business must stand out—not just in a good way, but in the right way.

List 3 or more people that stand out and make a great impression and what is it about that person that makes them stand out?

_____

_____

_____

_____

_____

_____

_____

_____

_____

_____

_____

_____

_____

_____

_____

_____

_____

_____

_____

_____

_____

_____

_____

_____

CALL IT A **CLAN**
CALL IT A **NETWORK**
CALL IT A **TRIBE**
CALL IT A **FAMILY**
WHATEVER YOU CALL IT
WHOEVER YOU ARE
YOU NEED ONE.

CHAPTER 10

YOUR NETWORK DETERMINES YOUR NET WORTH

NO MATTER WHAT industry you are in, it is very unlikely that you will be the only company in that industry. If there are no competitors, it may indicate that this is a market that's not worthwhile. There will be rival firms to consider, but there will also be suppliers and firms you can work alongside. There may be products that will complement your range, and working with these firms and individuals can boost your business.

Successful networking can be difficult. Quite often, you don't know the best places to network. This is why you should always be on the lookout for business conferences or major events. No matter what industry you are in, you are likely to find a major event where businesses of all shapes and sizes attend. This is a brilliant way to find out more about your industry and what changes may take place in the next couple of years within the industry.

Increased Business

A very obvious benefit of networking is increased business. If you are able to meet people who need your service, this is the ideal way for you to showcase what you have to offer. Networking with professionals at these events can set your business up for long-term success and opportunities.

More Opportunities

Before you get to the stage where you are gaining more business, you should recognize that you have a lot more opportunities available to you. Maybe you were unaware of these opportunities, or you didn't know how to get started. When you attend an event of this nature, there are plenty of new, unexpected opportunities available to you. Your ability to maximize on the connections you make at these events will really help push your business forward.

Connections Matter

One of the most important things to remember about business networking is that it isn't just for today, tomorrow or the near future. You can meet people that will help you later down the line. It's good to connect with people, even if there is no immediate chance of conducting business. It's important to build allies and friendships within your

industry. The more connections you have, the better con-
nected you'll be.

GET ADVICE

One of the greatest things to remember about business
is that someone else has already been in your position.
Other business owners have already gone through what
you may be currently going through; you can learn from
their mistakes. If you attend a major business event, do
your best to meet people who can offer you sound advice
and guidance.

Sometimes, just being in a room and making a positive
impression may be the entire reason for your attendance.
If you are looking to increase your profile, personally or
professionally, it makes sense to put yourself in a position
where you are seen. Attending networking events is vital
because that is the quickest way to make yourself known
amongst the right people in your industry. Attending these
events helps you learn that people from other companies
are just like you.

As my friend Pam Perry, PR guru and professional
would say, "Those who show up, go up!" This will develop
your confidence and help you see that there is nothing
magical or special about the people involved. They are
all hard-working people, hopefully like yourself. It can be
called various things, but the general term for the higher

ups is the "upline," meaning the people above you. How supportive are they? Do they call you? Do they help you put a plan in place? Are they as committed to your success as they are to their own? You should be able to relate to the people in your upline and be able to call them at any time to say, "I need some help."

The amount of support you have from the people above you is very important. When someone introduces a new person to an industry, then that person gets so busy bringing in other people that they don't teach and train the new person, the new person is considered an "orphan." You should spend at least 30 days helping a new person get integrated into the industry--training them, supporting them, and holding their hand until they feel confident enough to operate on their own. This is really about building long-term relationships. It's not just about bringing people into the business and moving forward. It's about working with these people and helping them to develop relationships.

Many people use the internet as their main networking tool. You can set up your website with autoresponders so that when you capture leads, the autoresponder follows up with subscribers. One of the greatest keys to success is follow-up, and automation allows a much more consistent method of following up.

List People that you would like to network with.

_____

_____

_____

_____

_____

_____

_____

_____

_____

_____

_____

_____

_____

_____

_____

_____

_____

_____

_____

_____

_____

_____

_____

_____

_____

_____

_____

_____

" SUCCESS ALL DEPENDS ON THE SECOND LETTER. "

CHAPTER 11

FOLLOW YOUR PASSION, NOT A PAYCHECK

"What's money? A man is a success if he gets up in the morning and goes to bed at night and in between does what he wants to do."

BOB DYLAN

WONDERING HOW TO follow your passion and succeed? The hardest thing for most people is to figure out what they want. Most people go through their entire lives without knowing their true purpose. Truthfully, you're the only one who can determine what you want and what your purpose in life is. However, the following three strategies can assist you in the process.

First, list all of the things you love doing, those things you can do over and over again, without ever getting bored. From this list, highlight the things that you are actually good at. If you love playing golf, but you're not very good at it, you won't be very successful at it. From the list of things that you love doing, figure out the ones that are your core strengths. Next, figure out how to provide value to people around you by doing what you are good at and what you love.

People don't care about what you do; they care about what you can do *for them*. It's important that people value you and your service or product enough to pay you well for it. Mere appreciation or hand claps don't yield a career. So, do what you love. Do what you are good at, and provide a value to people that can't be denied. Make sure the industry you are in appreciates you enough to pay you well or has great paying prospects *over time*.

Now, should you continue to follow your passion, even if it doesn't seem to offer any tangible rewards? Yes, only if you are absolutely certain you cannot live without it. In 2006, I ran for State Senate. I wanted to be a lawmaker and have a voice for those who couldn't speak for themselves, such as children and seniors. I wanted to make a difference. There were four people in the race. I came in second place and the incumbent retained the seat.

In life, sometimes you win and sometimes you lose. If you are passionate about an issue, pursue it. Even though I lost the race, I gained in other ways. People saw my passion and I was asked to work on other important issues that made a difference in the community. That was a learning experience and the ground work to do greater things.

If it is something without which you will live a life of regret and incompleteness, you should continue to follow it. If it is something that you are prepared to struggle for your entire life, understand that the big pay off may never happen. But, if you are still fiercely dedicated to take the risk, keep doing what you do. If the pain of quitting is greater than the pain of unrewarded hard work, keep pushing on.

Without passion, life has no meaning. You will be a living robot, going through a terminal disease called an aimless life. When you follow your passion, you may not get an easy life, but you will gain a fulfilled life.

HERE ARE SOME KEYS TO MAXIMIZING YOUR PASSION:

- When you follow your passion, you have to do so smartly. If you are misinformed, you may be heading for a life of heartbreak and despair.
- Ask questions instead of drawing conclusions. Questions lead to growth and expansion; conclusions lead to dead ends. Ask yourself: "What am I thinking? What else is possible? Would I love this? Why?"
- Ensure that your industry pays you enough to make a decent living, doing what you love over time. If not, then change tracks. You can grow to hate what you once loved if it does not love you back.

- The only exception to the above rule is if you have fallen so much in love with a career that you cannot live without it. Do this only if you fully understand the risk and the consequences, but are still willing to embrace it.
- Create a "passion plan" comprised of companies that pique your interest, job descriptions that sound like fun, and specific functions you would enjoy at a job. Then, determine where to look, what additional training you may need, which companies to contact, and what people to add to your network.
- Structure your time so that you work 40 hours, but budget 20 additional hours outside of your job to:
  - Assemble your passion plan.
  - Develop and refine your brand (LinkedIn profile, résumé, etc.).
  - Network. Take bold actions, like making the calls you've always feared and developing ways to stand out from the crowd.
- Identify patterns and themes in your life. What do others come to you for advice about? What comes as easily as breathing to you, but is a struggle for others?

Most importantly, make your life about always being true to who you are--not who or what family, friends, teachers and society tell you that you should be. Only then will you find your passion. The more aligned your thoughts and beliefs are to your purpose and passion, the easier it becomes to make decisions, set and achieve goals, and avoid fatigue.

Create a passion plan.

_____

_____

_____

_____

_____

_____

_____

_____

_____

_____

_____

_____

_____

_____

_____

_____

_____

_____

_____

_____

_____

_____

_____

_____

GOOD MUSIC DOESN'T HAVE AN EXPIRATION DATE.

CHAPTER 12

GET MOTIVATED

Music can inspire us and change our mood in a matter of minutes. Just like some ballads can make you sad or nostalgic, upbeat, inspiring songs can make you feel stronger, energized and ready to conquer the world.

Here is a playlist of motivational songs that get me going.

These songs range from R&B and country to inspirational, motivational tunes for females by females:

1. Whitney Houston: *I'm Every Woman*
2. Katy Perry: *Firework*
3. Kelly Price: *It's My Time*
4. Mary J. Blige: *Just Fine*
5. Jill Scott: *Golden*
6. Madonna: *Express Yourself*
7. Mariah Carey: *Hero*
8. Gloria Gaynor: *I Will Survive*
9. Alicia Keys: *This Girl is on Fire*
10. Aretha Franklin: *Respect*

11. Wilson Philips: *Hold On*
12. Queen Latifah: *U.N.I.T.Y.*
13. Shania Twain: *Man, I Feel Like a Woman*
14. Destiny's Child: *Independent Women*
15. Jamie O'Neal: *Somebody's Hero*
16. Christina Aguilera: *Beautiful*
17. Reba McEntire: *I'm a Survivor*
18. Mary Mary: *Go Get It*
19. Eve: *Who's That Girl?*
20. Miley Cyrus: *The Climb*

HABITS OF SUCCESSFUL PEOPLE

Rich people plan for four generations; poor people plan for Saturday night.

Here are some habits of successful people:

- They write down goals.
- They think long-term.
- They make a to-do list, with step-by-step actions to reach their goals.
- They know their purpose and mission.
- They want others to succeed; they are not haters.
- They spend time with the right people. It's important to have a mentor or associate with those who knows more than you.
- They accept responsibility for their failures.
- They don't blame others for their mistakes.
- They take risks.

- They stay humble.
- They share information and data.
- They exude joy.
- They embrace change.
- They talk about ideas.

"Success leaves clues. Study people you admire or want to be like."

TONY ROBBINS

According to *Forbes* magazine, there are 14 things successful people do on the weekends:

1. Make time for family and friends
2. Exercise
3. Pursue a passion
4. Vacation
5. Disconnect; no cell phones
6. Volunteer
7. Avoid chores
8. Plan
9. Socialize
10. Network
11. Reflect
12. Meditate
13. Recharge
14. Attend theatre, opera or sporting events

Many successful people participate in fundraising events. This is a great way to network and to meet others with similar interests. The visiblility also helps brand a successful person as philanthropic.

Successful people make decsions based on where they want to be, while unsuccessful people make decsions based on their current situation. Successful people are always looking for opportunities to help others.

According to Richard Branson, a business magnate, investor and philanthropist, some entreprenuers only think about making a lot of money. But it's much more effective for entrepreneurs to think about how they can improve the lives of others. If you get it right, the money will come. I truly believe that statement. I created Jackets for Jobs to make people's lives better, and yes the money came. I always say, "There's good ideas, and then there are God ideas." Jackets for Jobs was a *God idea*.

Success can be defined in many ways to many people. But when one mentions financial success, you have to think of Warren Buffet. He is the most successful investor in the world—maybe of all time.

What is the theme for your life?

_____
_____
_____
_____
_____
_____
_____
_____
_____
_____
_____
_____
_____
_____
_____
_____
_____
_____
_____
_____
_____
_____
_____
_____
_____

" If you want
to be more
powerful in
life, educate
yourself. "

It is that simple.

CHAPTER 13

KNOWLEDGE IS POWER

As THE OLD adage goes, "Knowledge is power." Everyone should have a library of books. We all need a diverse literary palate. Since this book focuses on goals and success, I've listed 10 books I have in my library that I would like to suggest you add to yours.

The Purpose Driven Life
What on Earth Am I Here For?
By Rick Warren

Do You!
12 Laws to Access the Power in You to Achieve Happiness and Success
By Russell Simmons

Girl, Make Your Money Grow!
A Sister's Guide to Providing Your Future and Enriching Your Life
By Glinda Bridgforth and Gail Perry-Mason

ALISON VAUGHN

It's Your Time
Activate Your Faith, Achieve Your Dreams and Increase in God's Favor
By Joel Osteen

Jump
Take the Leap of Faith to Achieve Your Life of Abundance
By Steve Harvey

How to Win Friends and Influence People
By Dale Carnegie

Holy Bible
The Power of God's Word for Everyday Living
The New International Version (NIV) is easy to read.

The Power of Broke
How Empty Pockets, A Tight Budget, and a Hunger for Success Can Become Your Greatest Competitive Advantage
By Daymond John

Lean In: Women, Work and the Will to Lead
By Sheryl Sandberg

Inspired Style
Co-authored by Alison Vaughn and other Top Image
Experts
This was my first book.

The phrase
"do not be afraid"
is written in the
bible 365 times.
That's a daily
reminder from
God to live
every day being
fearless.

CHAPTER 14

PRAYERS FOR YOUR BUSINESS AND SUCCESS

As a business owner, prayer is part of my daily ritual. God is the founder of my business, and He has asked me to oversee the daily operations. When I set goals and go through growth spells, God is there with me. I can only see what's in front of me, but God can see further ahead. God has big plans for us. He wants to see us succeed and He gets pleasure from our success.

Here are a few Scriptures, captured from the New International Version, you can read to help prosper your way.

GOD, MAY THE WORK I DO GLORIFY YOU.

In the same way, let your light shine before others, that they may see your good deeds and glorify your Father in heaven.

MATTHEW 5:16

GOD, CONTINUE TO SHOW YOUR FAVOR IN MY BUSINESS.

Surely, Lord, you bless the righteous; you surround them with your favor as with a shield.

PSALM 5:12

Ask God to show favor and provision in your business. God's favor doesn't just mean more money; it could mean new connections or witty inventions.

GOD, THANK YOU FOR WHAT YOU HAVE DONE AND FOR ALL YOU WILL DO IN MY BUSINESS.

Give thanks to the LORD, for he is good; his love endures forever.

PSALM 107:1

Remember I talked about "Please" and "Thank you" in chapter two. We come to God asking for so many things, but we can't forget to thank Him! Thank Him for past, current and future provision and favor.

GOD, OPEN MY EYES TO THE OPPORTUNITIES YOU'VE
PLACED BEFORE ME.

> *Be wise in the way you act toward outsiders;*
> *make the most of every opportunity.*

COLOSSIANS 4:5

Sometimes, as business owners, we wear blinders and we
can't see what He's placed before us. It may just be another
email in your inbox, a tweet, or a phone number that you
don't recognize. But God could be strategically placing a
life-changing opportunity before you.

When the producer called me to appear on Oprah's
show, I didn't recognize the phone number, but I still an-
swered. Just think if I had done like many people do when
they don't recognize a number—most people don't answer.
That unanswered call could have been a missed opportunity. I thank God for opening my heart to opportunities.

GOD WILL HELP YOU TO BECOME WEALTHY.

> *Remember the Lord your God, for it is he who*
> *gives you the ability to produce wealth.*

DEUTERONOMY 8:18

PRAYER IS
THE MOST
IMPORTANT
CONVERSATION
OF YOUR DAY.
TAKE IT TO GOD
BEFORE YOU
TAKE IT TO
ANYONE ELSE!

A Prayer for Prosperity and Financial Blessings

Father, it is your desire for us to prosper in all that we do. We speak forth promotions, business ideas, divine connections and partnerships. We stir up the same creative spirit that made the heavens and the Earth, to bring forth new ideas and inventions for the betterment of this world, that we can be a blessing to many.

ABOUT THE AUTHOR

ALISON VAUGHN, A Goldman Sachs Scholar, serves as the award-winning CEO of Jackets for Jobs, a Detroit-based non-profit organization. Jackets for Jobs is known by ABC's *"The View"*, NBC's *"Today Show"* and **NASDAQ** as a worthy organization to support. For more than two decades, she's worked diligently to cultivate the success of others through etiquette and grooming tips, as well as providing professional clothing to job seekers.

As a graduate of The Women's Campaign School at Yale University, she has secured millions of dollars for her company and is committed to sharing her first-hand knowledge with other business owners—allowing them to maximize profits and partnerships. In addition to mentoring business owners on how to stand out amongst the crowd, she doesn't mind sharing industry secrets she's used to position herself in boardrooms with billionaires across the nation.

Vaughn is a sought-after public speaker nationally and internationally. In the fall of 2014, she was chosen to speak at the World Islamic Economic Forum in Dubai, UAE on the rise of women entrepreneurs. Vaughn has inspired audiences with her insights on advocacy, entrepreneurism, empowerment and workforce development including area churches, civil rights organizations, corporations and non-profits, conference attendees, schools and universities and women's groups.

Alison's first book, *Inspired Style* in which she co-authored with other top image experts shares tips to help women look and be their best. She has also contributed articles on image, style and business etiquette for local newspapers.

She has received numerous accolades, "Entrepreneur of the Year" by Alabama A & M University, and "Businesswoman of the Year" by the National Association of Negro Business & Professional Business Women. The Michigan Chronicle honored Vaughn as a Woman of Excellence, and National Association of Women Business Owners (NAWBO) presented her with the Global Business Woman Award. **www. AlisonVaughn.com**

Made in the USA
Lexington, KY
03 October 2017